American ★ ★ ★ Symbols

by Vita Richman

Scott Foresman
is an imprint of

PEARSON

Glenview, Illinois • Boston, Massachusetts • Mesa, Arizona
Shoreview, Minnesota • Upper Saddle River, New Jersey

Every effort has been made to secure permission and provide appropriate credit for photographic material. The publisher deeply regrets any omission and pledges to correct errors called to its attention in subsequent editions.

Unless otherwise acknowledged, all photographs are the property of Pearson.

Photo locations denoted as follows: Top (T), Center (C), Bottom (B), Left (L), Right (R), Background (Bkgd)

Opener: Getty Royalty; 1 Getty Royalty; 3 Getty Royalty, Fotosearch.com; 4 Comstock; 5 Getty Royalty; 6 Getty Royalty, Image Farm; 7 SuperStock; 8 Getty Royalty, Comstock; 9 Image Farm, Getty Royalty, Fotosearch.com; 10 Getty Royalty, Comstock; 11 Comstock; 12 Getty Royalty, Image Farm

ISBN 13: 978-0-328-39700-6
ISBN 10:   0-328-39700-8

1 2 3 4 5 6 7 8 9 10 V010 17 16 15 14 13 12 11 10 09 08

What do you imagine when you think about the Fourth of July? Is it the flags waving in the wind? Is it the parade? Or the marching bands? Is it the family barbecue and the fireworks?

The Fourth of July is a great holiday in the United States. It is a birthday party for our country. It is on the day America decided to be free from England. This happened more than two hundred years ago, on July 4, 1776.

The first celebration of the Fourth of July took place in Massachusetts in 1781. Now you can see celebrations all over our country. Bands play. Fireworks light up the sky.

The flag is an important symbol of our country. A symbol is an image used to remind you of something. The flag reminds us of the United States. One of its nicknames is the Stars and Stripes.

Another symbol of our country is Uncle Sam. He wears a top hat, a vest, and a long jacket. He has stars on his hat. His trousers are striped. Sometimes people dress up like Uncle Sam in parades.

This man is dressed as Uncle Sam. People also draw Uncle Sam as a cartoon.

The Liberty Bell is a symbol of freedom. It is in Philadelphia at Independence Hall. The Liberty Bell was made in 1752. It cracked when it was rung for the first time! This bell had to be remade two more times. The last bell was rung for the final time in 1846. It cracked too much to fix.

Liberty Bell